Hawaii

"Learn about America in a beautiful way."

Beautiful America Publishing Company

The nation's foremost publisher of quality color photography

Current Books

Alaska	Maryland	Oregon Vol. II
Arizona	Massachusetts	Oregon Coast
Boston	Michigan	Oregon Country
British Columbia	Michigan Vol. II	Pacific Coast
California	Minnesota	Pennsylvania
California Vol. II	Missouri	Pittsburgh
California Coast	Montana	San Diego
California Desert	Montana Vol. II	San Francisco
California Missions	Monterey Peninsula	San Juan Islands
California Mountains	Mormon	Seattle
Chicago	Mt. Hood (Oregon)	Tennessee
Colorado	Nevada	Texas
Dallas	New Jersey	Utah
Delaware	New Mexico	Utah Country
Denver	New York	Vancouver U.S.A.
Florida	New York City	Vermont
Georgia	Northern California	Virginia
Hawaii	Northern California Vol. II	Volcano Mt. St. Helens
Idaho	North Carolina	Washington
Illinois	North Idaho	Washington Vol. II
Indiana	Ohio	Washington, D.C.
Kentucky	Oklahoma	Wisconsin
Las Vegas	Orange County	Wyoming
Los Angeles	Oregon	Yosemite National Park

Forthcoming Books

Alabama	Kauai	Oahu
Arkansas	Maine	Phoenix
Baltimore	Maui	Rhode Island
Connecticut	Mississippi	Rocky Mountains
Detroit	New England	South Carolina
The Great Lakes	New Hampshire	South Dakota
Houston	North Dakota	West Virginia
Kansas		

Large Format, Hardbound Books

Beautiful America	Beauty of Washington	Volcanoes of the West
Beauty of California	Glory of Nature's Form	Western Impressions
Beauty of Oregon	Lewis & Clark Country	Los Angeles, 200 Years

For a complete product catalog, send $1.00.
Beautiful America Publishing Company
P.O. Box 608
Beaverton, Oregon 97075

Hawaii

Concept and Design: Robert D. Shangle
Text: Paul M. Lewis
Featuring Ray Atkeson and David Muench Photography

Fifth Printing June, 1980
Published by Beautiful America Publishing Company
P.O. Box 608, Beaverton, Oregon 97075
Robert D. Shangle, Publisher

Library of Congress # 78-102325
ISBN 0-915796-16-3 (Hardbound)
ISBN 0-915796-15-5 (Softbound)

RAY ATKESON

Ray Atkeson has photographed Oregon and the Pacific Northwest for more than thirty years. He was born in the Midwest and spent his early years in Illinois and Missouri. So the Northwest is all the more exciting to him for the comparisons he is able to draw with other areas.

When he moved to the Northwest he became a photographer for a commercial studio in Portland. On weekends he roamed the Northwest with his camera. His early work was purchased by national publications and newspapers such as The New York Times, The Kansas City Star, The Houston Chronicle, and The London Illustrated News.

Since 1946 his work has appeared frequently in Holiday, Time, Sports Illustrated, National Geographic, and many other publications of national and international reputation.

DAVID MUENCH

David Muench received his early training from his father, the distinguished photographer of nature, Josef Muench. For several years young David accompanied the elder Muench on trips through the West, receiving thereby an incomparable education in landscape photography.

His enduring love for nature gained on these early excursions is reflected in his photography, regularly published in magazines like ARIZONA HIGHWAYS, NATIONAL WILDLIFE, and AUDUBON. David's work has also appeared in books, calendars, and other publications.

Printed by
Universal Color Corporation
Beaverton, Oregon

CONTENTS

INTRODUCTION

A few volcanoes that pushed up above the surface of the north Pacific some millions of years ago happened to do so in a part of the world where the weather could hardly be improved upon. Such, at least, is the happy situation now in these mid-ocean volcano tops that have come to be known as the Hawaiian Islands. In one sense, the salubrious climate made Hawaii what it is today. The Polynesians found it agreeable when they stumbled onto it a thousand or so years ago; and the modern-day Hawaiians, Chinese, Japanese, Filipino, Portuguese, Anglos, etc., etc., who live here apparently do not object to the soft, balmy air that bathes the islands in all seasons. The 50th state of the United States may just owe its statehood to its mean annual temperature in the 70s.

Beneficent trade winds that air-condition the islands also bring rain clouds over the windward slopes, causing a great deal of pineapple-and sugar-cane-growing moisture, and making possible a diversified agriculture. Hawaii is pretty much self-sufficient in food, and that's about all. It must import most of the other commodities it uses, from steel and lumber for construction to the myriad finished products necessary for modern societies, even those on tropical islands. To help pay for all this, the crafty islanders have gone into the resort business. And that gets us back to Hawaii's lovely, liveable climate, perhaps the most important reason why people are drawn here. The process of luring tourists and prospective residents to Hawaii's shores has proceeded apace since the introduction of super-duper jet aircraft and cut-rate fares. Getting people from other places to spend their money in the Islands has become such a basic industry that the future of Hawaii can hardly be imagined without this giant spur to its economy.

It has been said that human occupancy of Hawaii has increased rather than diminished its charm and liveability. This is true in a restricted sense. A great many of the ornamental and food plants that flourish in these benign climes were introduced by man, augmenting the limited range of vegetation brought in seed form over eons of time by the winds and by birds. On the other hand, man has introduced animal species with some unfortunate results, such as damage to habitats of native fauna. The great herds of goats in the two national parks (Haleakala and Hawaiian Volcanoes) come immediately to mind. Some conservationists believe the goats and other exotics constitute a grave danger for the Islands' endangered species.

The exotic species that is, without question, the biggest threat is man himself. Like goats and rabbits he is good at increasing his kind. In addition, he has the fearsome power to mold his environment into something it was not when he first arrived. So the combination of human numbers and human restlessness operating in an island setting could, if not checked, change Hawaii forever. Already, human encroachment on animal and bird habitats in nearly all of the islands has brought some rare creatures to the edge of extinction.

Perhaps a book of beautiful color photographs can make a point more forcefully through its pictorial content than by talking the subject to death. So I fall silent and give you leave to turn the pages. The samples of Hawaii's extravagant beauty depicted by the photographic artistry of David Muench and Ray Atkeson in the pages that follow may convince you that ''slow and easy'' is not only a well-known aspect of the Hawaiian life-style. It is also a good formula to remember if development of these marvelous islands is to stop short of exploitation.

P.M.L.

THE BIG ISLAND

Like the oversize head of a loosely joined sea serpent, Hawaii, the Big Island, forms the southeast vanguard of the chain. It is the biggest and youngest island, and still growing. Its size, give or take the last few lava flows, is about the same as Connecticut's. Vertically speaking, it is also Number One. Two of the five volcanoes that originally formed the Big Island top any other Hawaiian peaks. Mauna Kea and Mauna Loa are both just under 14,000 feet. Mauna Kea is slightly taller, is quiescent, and acquires a snowy summit in some seasons. Its name means "white mountain." Mauna Loa — "Long Mountain" — is still reluctant to go to sleep. Its last fiery hiccough was in 1950, less than a sneeze ago in geologic time. Like its tall sister, Mauna Loa is bulky — the most massive active volcano in the world. If it gets excited again, the world will know about it.

Like a festering boil on Mauna Loa's flank, the volcano Kilauea erupts frequently and is constantly seething. Its firepit, Halemaumau, keeps a super-hot stew going at about 2,000 degrees Fahrenheit. Bubbles form and break constantly on its floor and whirling clouds of steam rise from its half-mile-wide maw. Here is how *Science News* reported an impressive eruption in November 1967:

> Red-orange fountains of lava that boiled 200 feet high from Hawaii's Kilauea last week were less than a complete surprise . . . Minor earthquakes had been recorded as often as 200 to 400 a day in late October, and Kilauea's summit had puffed up to a size greater than ever recorded as molten rock flowed up from reservoirs some 25 to 40 miles below the earth's surface. The eruptions began about 2:30 a.m. November 5, with skyrocketing fountains of flaming lava, pumice and fumes. Lava spurted out at the rate of about 2 million cubic yards per hour, forming a lava lake 160 feet deep at the bottom of the 500-foot crater. About 35 million cubic yards of lava poured out before the eruption died 23 hours later . . .

Gently sloping volcanoes like Mauna Loa and Kilauea are relatively well behaved even when angry. Their very hot, fast-flowing lavas spill out quietly. Which is not to say volcano-watchers can loiter in Kilauea's caldera (the crater floor) when Halemaumau begins huffing and puffing. Sometimes the lava fountains reach terrifying heights — almost 2,000 feet in a 1959 eruption. But people can, and do, get close enough to see all of the awesome show as it bursts from the earth's molten interior.

Hawaii Volcanoes National Park, established in 1916 and including a coastal section added more recently, protects this volcanic terrain, including its east-slope rain forests and rare plants and birds. The National Park Service has established hiking trails for both the timid and venturesome hiker, including one to Halemaumau itself. The area is a wonderland of sinister steaming cracks, smelly mounds of steaming sulphur, forests of giant fern, lehua trees with their red flowers, and the sounds of Hawaii's unique honeycreeper, a bird that has a severely restricted habitat, even within the islands. Kilauea has its own hotel, perched on the rim of the crater. Called Volcano House, and established by an enterprising Greek some time ago, it has hot water and steam facilities furnished gratis by the volcano itself. Pele, the legendary Hawaiian goddess of volcanoes, is supposed to be seen sometimes hanging around the 'ohi'a forest between the hotel and Halemaumau. Someday she may decide to present a hot-water bill to the hotel management.

(Opposite:) The Kalalau overlook forms a background for ohia lehua blooms in Kauai's Napali wilderness.

If we could hover over the Big Island at a height sufficient to give us a view of the whole land mass we would see an astonishing variety of landscapes. From its (mostly) black sand beaches to its towering volcanoes there is also a variety of climates: balmy and dry with the soft air of the Kailua-Kona coast on the west; bracing in the high valleys of the volcano region; rainy and stormy on the windward Puna coast. More than the other Hawaiian Islands, the Big Island departs from the commonly accepted vision of tropical islands. Along much of its coast high cliffs challenge the sea, dropping waterfalls down their steep faces. It is not reef-encircled, in the manner of well-behaved tropical islands; it has, indeed, very little offshore reef at all. The Big Island is believed to be the first landing place of those courageous early Polynesian explorers who had navigated thousands of miles of ocean to find these tiny specks in the Pacific. What a magnificent and surprising sight must have been Hawaii's powerful coastal cliffs and majestic cascades! And the fiery breath of a volcano lighting up the night sky and shaking the earth underfoot! Small wonder that the cult of Pele quickly claimed the allegiance of those early settlers.

The mystery and awe that permeated the daily lives of the first Hawaiians must have been continually reinforced by the powerful contrasts encountered on the biggest and youngest island. Tradition is still a force that lives in harmony with Hawaii's contemporary impulse. The Kamaainas — Hawaii's old aristocracy — lament the disappearance of the ''old'' Hawaii, but this spirit still lives on the Big Island. Physically, it is much the same as it was when those early Tahitians made landfall there about the middle of the eighth century A.D. Like all of the islands with any kind of mountain ridge, it has a wet side and a dry side, with tropical jungles on the one hand and sandy desert areas on the other. There are fern-tree rain forests, dry prairies and grazing country, black-sand beaches and white-sand beaches, the wild, sea-lashed, and ever-changing coastline of the Puna district on the east, and the sweet, balmy air and waters of the so-called ''Kona Coast,'' an increasingly popular resort region for tourists, comprising about 60 miles of the coastal slopes of Mauna Loa and Hualalei.

''Kona,'' for many visitors, is the town of Kailua and its nearby hotel area of Keauhou. Although the Big Island has long been the least developed, that is changing. The Kona area and just about the entire western coast of Hawaii is included on the schedules of most visitors to the Islands, and that's where man-made rearrangements of the landscape are happening. So far the building has been low-key, with obvious thought given to blending environmental and esthetic considerations with the more immediately practical one of making a profit. But now that Hilo, the Big Island's big city, is served by direct passenger jets from the mainland (since the late 1960s) more and more thousands of visitors will continue to discover Hawaii's uncluttered charm and mystery.

A Kona landmark is the City of Refuge, one of several established in the islands before western civilization arrived. The Kona sanctuary, on the shore of Honaunau Bay, 20 miles south of Kailua, was built by Kamehameha, and is the most important such refuge historically. Before the Hawaiians came under the influence of Christianity, the cities of refuge were established as havens for lawbreakers and for those vanquished in war. The temple of Kona's refuge was built about 1650, but razed early in the 19th century after the old religions had been rejected. The City of Refuge National Historical Park was set up in 1961 and the temple was rebuilt. The fearsome wooden gods were carved again and set facing seaward on the original wall that still guards the haven on the land side. The stone wall is about 1,000 feet long, 12 feet high, and 17 feet thick. Its stones were fitted together perfectly, without mortar. The City of Refuge now offers sanctuary to Hawaii's endangered culture. Some of the ancient Hawaii building arts are still practiced there.

One of the best ways to "be" in a place is to camp out in it. The disadvantages are, of course, that camping requires some resoluteness of mind and a fairly sturdy constitution. But camping in the Islands' gentle climate is no hardship, and the rewarding intimacy with natural things that one can experience is overpayment for any inconvenience. One natural thing the camper will not experience in Hawaii is a snake. None of these reptiles is found on the Islands. Throughout the Islands there are about 70 parks and campgrounds, both state and county. Of the two Hawaiian national parks, one, Hawaiian Volcanoes National Park on the Big Island, has a campground somewhat in the manner of mainland ones. This is Kamoamoa, close to the national park visitors' center at Wahaula. The campground is situated within an immense *heiau* called *Moa* (chicken).

The county beach parks on Hawaii as on the other islands are delightful, esthetically fulfilling camping spots. They are quiet and beautiful. Their jungle-and-coast character makes them some of the most interesting places to be in Hawaii. And campers in Hawaii can travel light — important for bicyclers — because temperatures usually remain in the sixties, even at night. Unfortunately, mosquitoes do their vacationing here, too. There are several species of them. Nevertheless, camping is no hardship, and is the economical way to savor the "essence" of the islands without the competition of the tourist hordes who head for the highly organized (and expensive) pleasure palaces being developed on the Big Island wherever a white sand beach is available and the tropical breezes blow.

On Hawaii the camper can easily find his preferred spot. For example, several campgrounds line up along the southeast shoreline just below Hilo. These are Isaac Hall Beach Park; McKenzie State Park; and Harry K. Brown Beach Park, near the Kaimu black sand beach. On the island's lee side, along the Kona and South Kohala coasts, there is a wide choice of beach parks, such as Hapuna State Beach Park, preferred by most residents of the Big Island for its fine camping and swimming beach. The Kona and Kohala beaches are consistently dry and sunny, and the soft, tropical air builds up that south seas torpor that everyone comes to the Islands to find.

(Opposite:)
The Big Island's Kona Coast is the setting for the City of Refuge National Historical Park.

(Upper:)
The surf is up at Oahu's Sunset Beach, one of the world's greatest surfing beaches.

(Lower:)
Ohia and koa form a mixed rain forest vegetation in Kauai's Kokee State Park.

MOLOKAI AND LANAI

Molokai, which used to be "the island nobody knows," lately has edged into the limelight occupied by the "Big Four" — Hawaii, Maui, Oahu, and Kauai. Molokai has the biggest percentage of Hawaiians, fullblooded and otherwise. Its people still adhere to the old ways in their daily lives. They fish with their own woven nets, raise taro patches, and pound the taro roots for poi. They keep alive many of the native taboos, legends, and superstitions and live much as the Hawaiians did before Captain Cook came into the picture. It is reported that island *kahunas* (witch doctors) still do hexes on command, which makes the place almost as primitive as some back-country parts of the mainland.

The fifth largest Hawaiian island is 37 miles long and 10 miles wide. Its shoe shape results from two volcanoes choosing to line up next to each other as they rose from the sea. The West Molokai volcano was first, however, and this stretch of the island has leveled off to a plateau of some 1,300 feet. The eastern part is all jagged mountains and cliffs, except for the low plain of Kalaupapa Peninsula, where the once infamous leper colony still exists. It is no longer the place of mystery and exile it once was, where lepers were isolated to live out pitiful existences. New drugs have effectively checked the disease in the last quarter century, and those lepers still on Kalaupapa are there voluntarily. The colony was established in the midst of some of Molokai's most sumptuous scenery, a little nub of land cut off from the rest of Molokai by a steep mountain wall. Now, as before, no roads lead to it. But there's an airport, and mule trails down the mountain.

Molokai's lack of development is blamed, partly, on the inhibiting psychological factor of the leper colony. A more solid reason is the historical fact that the land was bought up by pineapple companies, which were not concerned with luring tourists. But there are signs now that Hawaii's energetically stage-managed tourist boom is reaching the Friendly Island. The southern shoreline will soon have resort facilities and residential development. And Kaunakakai, Molokai's principal town, will shortly be growing from very small to not so small, when hotels and homes go in on the south coast.

There's a rough, winding road along the southeast coast, connecting tiny coastal settlements squeezed between the sea and the mountains. The road goes on for about 30 miles until it reaches the eastern tip of the island by climbing over mountain ridges into Halawa Valley, most of which is now owned by the Puu O Hoku Ranch. Along much of the south shore are fine views of the islands of Maui and Lanai, and at Halawa itself, West Maui dominates the scene across the narrow interisland channel. Even the huge mass of Haleakala may be seen hulking in the background.

The dreamy quiet of Halawa Valley may not last much longer. A comprehensive tourist development, including a golf course and all the usual paraphernalia of tourism is planned at Puu O Hoku. Many little valleys cut into the high cliffs that rise out of Halawa. Its most eye-catching feature is probably Moaula Falls, dropping from a lofty cliff with great bravura into a lovely mountain pool.

The most spectacular coastline in the Islands — from Halawa to Kalaupapa — is unapproachable by road. There isn't any road. Awesome 2,000-foot, green cliffs and mighty waterfalls can be seen only from a boat or from the air. Interisland flights between Oahu and

Maui usually fly by this coast. Boat trips ashore at one of the few coastal valleys are possible in the summertime when the sea quiets down enough to permit going in close. These solitary valleys have no permanent residents. Only cliffs and caves and wind-whipped cascades — a great place to be alone. Well, not quite alone. A solitary wanderer here shares his solitude with deer, goats, wild boar, partridge, and maybe even a Hawaiian hunter or two intent on bagging a specimen of one of the foregoing.

Standing a few miles off West Maui's south coast is a hump of land that rises from the sea in a smooth curve on the south and gradually slopes down again to the north coast. It looks like an enormous whale idling in the strait. It's the island of Lanai.

Lanai is the sixth island in size, 17 miles long and 13 miles wide. Nearly all of it is in private hands — those of the Dole company, which, as everybody knows, turned the island from a barren rock to the champion pineapple grower of the world. But not all of it is in pineapples — just 15,000 acres, or one-sixth. A lot of the rest is shoreline, mountain slopes, forests, and desert. Visitors are hospitably received although facilities are limited to one small 10-room hotel in Lanai City. It's a far cry from the tourist palaces of Honolulu. Most of Lanai's population (about 3,000) work for Dole and live in Lanai City, which has one of the best climates in the Islands. Perched halfway up Lanai's mountain, it has cool summery days and cool nights, its iron-roofed houses sheltered by the evergreen arms of majestic pine trees imported from the mainland.

Westward down the hill from Lanai City is the island's harbor, at Kaumalapau, where pineapples are loaded onto barges. A six-mile road takes a winding course through pineapple fields to get there from Lanai City. North and south of Kaumalapau the coastline rises abruptly from the sea in headlands and cliffs. The south central coast is also served by a road from Lanai City, an eight-mile stretch that reaches Manele Bay and its small-boat harbor. Just around the point to the west is Hulopoe Bay, with a fine swimming beach. This is an area scheduled for recreational development, including hotel facilities on the high ground behind what will eventually be a unified park area including both Manele and Hulopoe bays.

On the way to Manele, the road passes close to some very well preserved rock carvings called the Luahiwa petroglyphs, about half a mile off on a dirt road. Several other points of historical interest in this area are reachable by rough trails fit only for four-wheel or two-legged drive. One of these places is Kaunolu Village, a National Historic Landmark, where the ruins of many former dwellings and other village artifacts of Kamehameha's time are preserved. The great king favored Kaunolu as a place to rest after he took on the wearisome job of lording it over all the Islands. Nearby, on the coast to the west, are the remains of Halulu Heiau; Kahekili's Jump, where warriors beating a retreat are believed to have taken a 62-foot dive into the sea from a low spot in the cliffs; and two miles away, Palikaholo, topping the rest of the coastline at 1,083 feet.

The northwestern part of Lanai is, in the main, a plain, with very little rain. Nothing much else here, either. More or less in the heart of this plateau, however, is a canyon called Garden of the Gods. If strange looking natural structures and multicolored lava walls are attributes of a garden, then this is that kind of place. Erosion by all the elements of wind, rain, and sun has fashioned some impressively grotesque lava sculptures looking like dejected late-stayers surveying the wreckage after a wild bacchanale. Like others of this little island's special places, the Garden is hard to find and easy to miss, without careful directions.

(Following Two Pages:) A patented Hawaiian sunset creates a spectacular tableau of palm trees and the little church of St. Peter on the Big Island's Kona Coast.

15

Lanai's highest point, Lanaihale (3,370 feet) is in the southeast interior. A hiking trail leads to it, as does also the Munro Trail, a dirt road named after George Munro, a New Zealand naturalist who preceded Mr. Dole and his pineapples and planted the ridge line with many tropical plants from his native land. Lanaihale is like a watchtower where all the Hawaiian Islands except Kauai are spread out like a kingdom before the watcher's enraptured gaze.

The Munro Trail goes for seven miles from the hills in southeast Lanai to Koele, in the open country of the west slopes near Lanai City. The road travels through a rain forest of pines and tropical exotics, also the work of the indefatiguable New Zealander.

Lanai's windward coast is quite lonely and nearly uninhabited. The northern part is a window onto Molikai, across a seven-mile channel. From the southeast coast (Halepalaoa Landing) West Maui comes into view. There's Shipwreck Beach, near the top of the island, a four-mile stretch littered with the remains of ships, including a few hulks. Keomuku, midway along the windward side, is an abandoned village with a photogenic old church surrounded by a grove of palm trees. Nearby are the ruins of a *heiau* and some more petroglyphs. Two parallel roads, mostly of sand and dirt, skim this shoreline for some 40 miles from Shipwreck Beach in the north to Naha in the south.

Man's ability to alter not only the landscape but the *feeling* of his habitat has sometimes caused the death of a locale's original and natural magic. This could easily happen to the small piece of volcanic dust that is called the island of Lanai, when tourist-oriented recreational projects now being planned and others still undreamed-of become a physical presence there. If good judgment and restraint are practiced by both private and public sectors, little injury to natural values will be visited upon the island. That is an outcome devoutly to be wished.

OAHU

For many people — tourists and would-be tourists — the island of Oahu is the city of Honolulu and that's all. For others the city of Honolulu is the beach at Waikiki. These attitudes have been a powerful force in transforming Waikiki from a thin worthless strip of sand backed by a rather dreary swamp into a thin, billion-dollar strip of sand backed by a jostling mob of high-rise hotels where tourists pay premium prices for rooms with an ocean view.

This essay won't be going into the pros and cons of Waikiki's continuing metamorphosis as this century goes by. Anybody who hasn't been living deep in the Brazilian jungles or at the bottom of a well for the past few years knows about the excited and sometimes angry discussions on both sides of what has been done at, and to, Waikiki in the name of tourism. Perhaps it is enough to say that the glittering hotel strip has created its own environment. Visually it is not the Hawaii of old; its glass and steel monoliths seem like an intrusion that blocks out the *real* Hawaii. Some of Honolulu's famous landmarks have been pushed into hiding by Waikiki's (and Honolulu's) vertical masses. But other things haven't changed. That soft and celebrated Hawaiian air is still there, with its mean annual temperature in the 70s, the sea still obligingly turns a brilliant blue at the dawn of each day, the breakers still shape themselves into the proper conformation for some of the best surfing anywhere, and the sunsets are still shamelessly gorgeous and flaming. There's a lot to do and see in Waikiki that isn't very restful in the south seas, slow-and-easy tradition. But a great many people like it that way.

Even before the high-rise hotels, Waikiki was a favorite vacation spot of Hawaii's royalty. The great Kamahameha may have had it in mind when he and his army dropped in from the Big Island in 1795, did an end run by landing at Maunalua Bay to the east, and pushed Oahu's warriors all the way to the Nuuanu Pali on the north, from which precipice they are said to have fallen to their deaths.

Oahu is the third largest island in area, 40 miles long and 26 miles wide. More than three-fourths of Hawaii's population live here. That's about one million persons, half in the capital city. Oahu was formed by two volcanoes, whose remains are represented in the two mountain ranges that run through the island — the Koolau Range from the northwest to the southeast, and the Waianae Mountains that form the west coast. The Waianaes have Oahu's highest peak: 4,030-foot Mt. Kaala.

Although Honolulu now sprawls almost all the way to the Pali, its outer fringes are pleasantly unobtrusive. Many of its private homes, churches, and even commercial and governmental buildings are visual assets. In the Makiki Heights area toward the Pali, to give an example, are Hawaii's most beautiful homes, some rivaling those in any other city of the world. Within the city proper are many architecturally stunning buildings, such as the modern State Capitol, on Hotel Street; the First Methodist Church of Honolulu on South Beretania Street; the Federal Building and Iolani Palace, both on King and Richards streets; and, in the old downtown section, among the decrepit remains of the city's oldest business buildings, the Kamehameha V Post Office, built in 1870.

Honolulu is really too complicated to summarize in a few sentences. For one thing, it is

(Following Two Pages:) Pandanus fronds frame a Kauai chef d'oeuvre, Lumahai Beach.

one of the world's most cosmopolitan cities. It has about 18 newspapers, in English, Japanese, Chinese, Filipino, and Korean. It has 200 churches, including Buddhist temples and Shinto shrines. And it has a Chinatown, naturally. All the accoutrements of a big, bustling, modern city are here as well as carefully preserved reminders of an earlier time. Two famous and prestigious schools of Honolulu — the Kamehameha Schools for children of Hawaiian ancestry, and the Punahou School for children of missionary forebears — carry on island traditions.

East from Waikiki, Kapiolani Park spreads out toward another familiar landmark: Diamond Head, an ancient crater once used for coastal defense. Private homes are spotted on its slopes, as are old gun emplacements. There's a road into the gigantic interior of the crater. And when the Hawaiian National Guard isn't using its firing range there, hikes are permitted to the seaward rim.

Punchbowl Crater and Pearl Harbor are too important to be left out of a selected list of Honolulu landmarks. Punchbowl, as most of us know, is now the National Memorial Cemetery of the Pacific, where long, long rows of markers honor some 21,000 war dead, from World War I through Vietnam. The crater overlooks downtown Honolulu and commands sweeping coastal and mountain views. Pearl Harbor is undergoing a revitalization program aimed at restoring its former fish ponds and oyster beds in addition to water fowl habitats, all lost when the strategic harbor was converted into an industrial and military site.

Even though the city and county of Honolulu now comprise all of Oahu, most of the island's population is concentrated in and around the city proper, so that it is possible to enjoy much of the island without having to look through thousands of people, their buildings, cars, and other toys. The eastern tip is becoming crowded but the western end, the Waianae highlands, and some of the north coast and windward side still offer areas that at least project a sense of isolation. One of these is the Waianae region dominated by the Waianae Mountains. This stretch is quite uncommercial. Few tourists get to it; visitors are mostly Hawaiians from other parts of the island. One of the best surfing beaches anywhere is at Makaha, and here there are extensive homes and tourist facilities. But the deeper Makaha Valley is being left in its natural state. This part of Oahu is also the driest, and its combination of mountainous terrain and fine beaches makes it a paradise for the lover of the outdoors. At about the midpoint of the Waianaes is Kolekole Pass, which can be driven *to* but not *through*. It offers exceptional views westward toward the sea and eastward to the Koolau Range over Leilehua Plateau. This cool plateau contains extremely fertile farm land, planted mostly in pineapple.

The north shore is also a fertile plain, switching lately from a sugar-growing economy to truck farming and resort facilities. While uncrowded now, this area will not long remain so. The same is true of windward Oahu, where the long line of the Koolaus raise their spectacular, fluted cliffs, or *palis*, along a narrow coastal plain. This is one of the most photogenic parts of Oahu, with its picturesque bays and many quiet beaches. Kaneohe Bay, largest on this coast, and windward terminus of the Nuuanu Pali highway, has marvelous coral gardens which may be viewed from glass-bottom boats. Kailua beach, near the eastern tip, is a superb swimming beach whose water is turquoise blue and whose waves are gentle. Kahaluu, a charming seaside village past Kaneohe Bay, used to engage in pineapple processing (its name was formerly Libbyville). At Hauula, about 10 miles away, are the Sacred Falls, a truly enchanted place. Here, in a gorge only 50 feet wide, the falls plunge 87 feet into a beautiful mountain pool. Visitors to this idyllic spot must work for their reward, though. To reach it involves a hot, one-mile climb to the ridge top. As a bonus, there's a matchless view of the natural beauty on all sides.

Also on the windward side, toward the north coast, is the settlement of Laie, a unique and beautiful example of what is possible when native groups and enlightened church leaders work hand in hand. Most of Laie's residents are Mormons of Hawaiian and Samoan extraction. They and the Mormon Church have developed about 6,000 acres into an integrated area reflecting Hawaii's south seas culture. The Polynesian Cultural Center is part of this, with replicas of the native villages of old Hawaii, Fiji, Tahiti, Samoa, Tonga, and the New Zealand Maoris. Cultural pageants are given for visitors, and native crafts are demonstrated. An impressive Mormon Temple has also been built here, along with a branch of Brigham Young University.

(Upper:) Subtle evening light brings flowing life to coco palms of Kona's City of Refuge National Historical Park.
(Lower:) Koolau Pali stands guard on Oahu's windward side.
(Opposite:) Wailua Falls is at the head of the Wailua River Valley on Kauai.

(Upper:)
  Gigantic Na Pali cliffs shelter Kauai's legend-rich Valley of the Lost Tribe.

(Lower:)
  Sunny Lahaina (Maui) and showery mountains collaborate in a rainbow.

(Opposite:)
  A tourist boat glides between the heavy vegetation of Kauai's Wailua River.

(Opposite:) Heavy surf laps at the lava cinders of Kalapana Black Sand Beach on the island of Hawaii.
(Upper:) The waters of Waikiki's celebrated beach glitter in the warm sun.
(Lower:) The snow-flecked cones of Mauna Kea on the Big Island are seen from the saddle road.
(Following Two Pages:) The Kona coastline spreads south from the Kohala highlands of Hawaii.
Beauty framed in beauty – a Hawaiian girl and hibiscus blossoms.

(Preceding Two Pages:) Ukampo Beach, leeward Oahu, here and on the cover, provides a poetic setting of almost impossible beauty in this blend of sea, sand, sky, mountains, and grassy groves.
(Upper:) A section of palm-fringed coastline on Hawaii is typical of the Big Island's wild beauty.
(Lower:) Kilauea Iki's crater spreads out to view in Hawaii Volcanoes National Park. Mauna Loa is in the background.
(Opposite:) Maui's Seven Sacred Pools are a popular attraction in the coastal section of Haleakala National Park. Two of the cascades and three of the pools are shown here.

(Preceding Two Pages:) Waialeale's ever-present clouds swirl away from the ramparts of Kauai's rain-drenched mountain and a warm, brilliant moment of sunshine bathes the Hanalei Valley. Banana trees in the foreground get their share, too.
(Upper:) A visit to Kauai's Fern Grotto is the climax of Wailua River scenic boat trips.
(Lower:) Kailua Beach Park, on windward Oahu, is a popular spot for swimmers and sailors.
(Opposite:) Iao Valley's famous Needle points a green finger to the Maui Sky.

(Upper:) A Hawaiian luau calls for extensive preparation. Here the "table" is being set with colorful decorations and tasty tropical foods.
(Lower:) Many smokes attest to the nervous disposition of Hawaii's Kilauea, the "drive-in" volcano.
(Opposite:) Live pahoehoe lava glows a menacing red at Kaena Pt., Hawaii Volcanoes National Park.

(*Opposite:*) *The sea beats against the rugged headlands of the Na Pali coast, seen here at Ke'e Beach, Kauai.*
(*Upper:*) *Boardwalk (Devastation Trail) goes through a skeleton forest fashioned by Kilauea Iki eruption in 1959.*
(*Lower:*) *Pineapple Hill, Maui, shows why it got its name. Molokai is across the channel.*

(Upper:)
   Porpoises leap and play in the clear water of Whaler's Cove at Oahu's Sea Life Park.

(Lower:)
   Clouds sweeping across the Big Island reflect the brilliant glow of an eruption of Mauna Ulu crater in Hawaii Volcanoes National Park.

(Opposite:)
   Kilauea's seething firepit, Halemaumau, is seen here from the rim of the volcano's crater. Amaumau fern occupies the foreground.

(Upper:)
  The big rollers at Oahu's Sunset Beach attract surfers from all over the world.

(Lower:)
  Cinder cones rise from the gigantic crater of Haleakala, in Haleakala National Park, Maui.

(Opposite:)
  Hibiscus blooms, Kailua-Kona.

(Preceding Two Pages:) The North Kohala coastline of the Big Island stretches into the distance, as seen from the Pololu overlook.
(Upper:) Smoking Halemaumau, Hawaii Volcanoes National Park, on the Big Island.
(Lower:) A colorful sunset silhouettes graceful palm trees on the Kona Coast of Hawaii.
(Opposite:) The Queen's Bath, a natural swimming hole along the Kalapana coastline of Hawaii, has a mix of ocean and fresh waters.

(Opposite:) A Waikiki sunset silhouettes palm trees and a thatched hut.
(Upper:) A sugar cane field on Maui.
(Lower:) Swaying palms frame a tableau of outrigger canoes and surfers at Waikiki Beach.

(Upper:) *Pleasure boats crowd the port of Lahaina, Maui.*
(Lower:) *Lone silversword plant grows amid the desolation of the 10,000-foot-high rim of Haleakala Crater. In the distance rise the mountains of West Maui.*
(Opposite:) *A cascade and tulip trees make a sumptuous setting on the Hamakua coast of Hawaii.*

(Opposite:) Spectacular Akaka Falls, a little north of Hilo on the Big Island, drop 420 feet into a mossy gorge.
(Upper:) Neat taro patches in the Wailua Valley invite the eye of the Hana Highway traveler on Maui's north coast.
(Lower:) Honolulu high-rise skyline is no match for Diamond Head, on the city's eastern fringes.

MAUI

Maui, after Oahu, is the best-known of the Hawaiian Islands. This may be due in no small measure to its place in history since the white man decided to rescue these bits of Pacific Ocean real estate from the natives. Lahaina, its earliest town, was a busy and boisterous whaling port in the last century. It is where New England whalers stopped over and were treated to the ultimate in Hawaiian hospitality — young, female version. It was also one of the first targets of the austere Boston missionaries who came to prepare the Hawaiians for entry into a Congregationalist paradise.

Maui has a funny-looking profile. There's a bulge on the east, and a bulge on the west, and an isthmus in between. It faintly resembles a dumbbell. But this analogy would surely not suit Maui residents. With considerable lack of modesty they show their pride in their island with the by now well-known slogan, *"Maui no ka oi,"* — "Maui is the Best." Maui, 729 square miles in extent, is the second island in size, after Hawaii. Originally two islands, it is composed of the West Maui mountains and environs, on one side of the isthmus, and enormous Haleakala, on the other. Puu Kukui, the West Maui summit (5,788 feet), is the second wettest spot in the Islands with more than 33 feet of rain a year.

Haleakala ("House of the Sun") is a very big (10,023 feet) and big-mouthed mountain. Its dormant crater — the volcano had a flank eruption back in 1790 — is so vast it could cradle Manhattan Island, bank debts and all. Centuries of erosion carved this immense hollow, and latter-day volcanism raised cones along its floor. The crater is really a high valley, 7½ miles long, 2½ miles wide, and 3,000 feet deep. It covers 19 square miles and is 21 miles in circumference. The summit of Haleakala was made a national park in 1961; it is one of two such parks in the islands, the other being Hawaii Volcanoes National Park on the Big Island.

A famous Haleakala trademark is the rare and beautiful silversword plant, believed to grow nowhere but on the mountain's crater. Its dazzling silver leaves have been likened to porcupine quills, or shimmering spikes. It is a yucca-like plant that after many years produces a six-foot stalk of purple and yellow flowers that bloom for about a week. Then the plant dies, after bequeathing its seed to the harsh cindery volcanic terrain where it grew. Nowadays there is a two-lane highway that winds around the volcano up to the rim of the crater. Before this road was built, visitors to the summit had to use leg or animal power; after making the difficult ascent, people would take silversword plants as souvenirs and payment for their efforts. The silversword quickly became, and still is, an endangered species. Now protected, it is making a comeback, guarded closely by the National Park Service.

Haleakala's bleak crater easily suggests a moonscape. From the House of the Sun Observatory, where the road leads, a visitor can gaze at its vast extent, and admire the subtle color changes of the nine cinder cones rising from it. This ruggedly beautiful landscape is best visited around sunrise or sunset. A hike or horseback ride along a portion of the 30 miles of trails in the crater can enhance enjoyment of a spectacle that is especially impressive when the sun is low on the mountain's horizon. The play of sun and clouds, for which Haleakala is famous, creates an enchanted world of constantly changing pastel hues on the cinder cones; giant shadows race across the silent basin, and sometimes the combination of sun and clouds or mist fashions a rainbow aureole.

The crater does, of course, contain havens of vegetation. There is lichen; mountain *pili* (related to a lowland plant once used for grass houses); native trees such as the sandalwood, and, in the wetter areas, the 'ohi'a; and ferns. The *nene*, a small Hawaiian goose that lives in the highlands, may occasionally be seen in these well-watered areas. Hikers can easily see most of Haleakala's variety of wonders by staying one or more nights in one of the Park Service's three free cabins and either letting the Service plan a trip for them or taking a conducted overnight hike (during summer). Human beings have left their works there, too; there are still the remains of some early Hawaiian structures such as stone altars, shelters, and wind barriers.

A recent addition to Haleakala National Park, a corridor of land called the Kipahula Valley, has been of immense value both in a scenic and scientific sense. The addition reaches from the upper southeast flank of Haleakala all the way to the eastern shore, including the coast's unique and spectacular Seven Sacred Pools. Being on the wet and windward side of the island, Kipahulu is a verdant wilderness paradise and one of the few spots in the islands where native species of flora and fauna are in the majority.

Maui's eastern shore is a reminder of old Hawaii. Although Hana, its focal point, has direct air service from Honolulu, it should be approached overland from Kahului. A scenic 50-mile drive from that airport town in Maui's ''neck'' reveals the charm of this secluded coast with its waterfalls, sheer cliffs, and sea. The spectacular vistas begin after Pauwela and continue on to at least the Seven Sacred Pools below Hana. The road is narrow and twisty, but that, of course, is why it's in such an extravagant setting. Superhighways don't get very intimate with the countryside they rip through. This part of the Maui coast is one of the flashiest shows that the showy Islands have to offer, and if driven along, should be done at a leisurely pace. The Hana Highway, as it is called, passes beach parks and campgrounds, threading its way around the sumptuous cliffs and clefts of the north Maui coast. Along the road's cliff-hanging route are pandanus trees and giant fern, and a lush, tropical jungle of 'ohi'a, *kukui*, *koa*, and paperbark trees. Waterfalls tumble down many of the folds in the rock wall. The towns on this coast are really only small clusters of houses, whose inhabitants are dependent on the land for their sustenance. For example, they still pound poi, as in former times. The little villages, like Keanae and Wailua, are off on side roads, and their inhabitants greet all visitors with unfailing friendliness and equally unfailing curiosity. They will even offer an outrigger canoe ride in the protected coves — the open surf on this coast is beautiful, but too wild and brutal for such excursions. At Wailua, a westward glance affords a stunning view of mighty Haleakala's Koolau Gap and the river of lava, stilled (and cooled) by time, thrown out by the volcano in one of her long-ago tantrums.

Four miles from Hana, at Waianapanapa State Park, are two lava tubes or caves (Waianapanapa and Waiomao caves) containing water and believed to be connected. This is a legend-haunted, romantic spot where a visitor can fish, swim, or just explore. The legend concerns a Hawaiian princess, murdered by her jealous husband who had pursued her to the caves. Her sighs and sobs can still be heard in the echoing reaches of the caves by those who listen carefully. Apparently the most exciting time to visit Waianapanapa is in April, the month of the murder; then the water turns red, the legend says.

Hana, sometimes called the Heavenly, is the *piece de resistance* of Maui's east coast. It is only lightly brushed by the modern world's intrusive presence. Hana is really the headquarters of a huge (15,000 acres) cattle ranch and luxury resort. It is home to a

(Upper:) Ki'i-god sculptures stand guard in the City of Refuge National Historical Park on Hawaii's Kona Coast.
(Lower:) Mauna Kea, Hawaii's tallest mountain, sits for a rare cloud-free portrait in this view from Hilo Bay.
(Opposite:) Like royal subjects, anthuriums crowd around a tiki image carved from a fern trunk on the Island of Hawaii.

thousand or so long-time residents — Hawaiians and part-Hawaiians employed in the ranch operations. Much that is Polynesian in culture is preserved in the Hana Valley, especially the vocal music, hula dancing, and native crafts. There is none of the ''resort'' atmosphere here; just the simple, priceless natural attributes that make Hana a unique place in the world. In spite of its relatively easy accessibility it is still unspoiled, a condition akin to a miracle in the era of frantic tourist promotion.

Wailuku, in the isthmus of Maui, is the county seat. It's an old town that still very much reflects the missionary influence in Maui, including a New England church and a museum of memorabilia named Hale Hoikeike. The museum is housed in an impressive building once part of Wailuku Female Seminary. The house has thick stone walls and exposed beams of sandalwood. The plaster on the walls has a rather unusual binding ingredient — human hair. Part of Wailuku's attraction is its pleasant mix of old and new in architecture and ambience. One of the older sections of the town is called Happy Valley, whose old wooden buildings now house respectable businesses, but whose name memorializes the happiness once generated by the ladies of this part of town.

Staid Wailuku and its more bustling ''sister'' town on the isthmus, Kahului, have about the same population (11,000-12,000). Kahului is the ''working'' city, the sea- and air port, the processing center for sugar, pineapple, and molasses produced by the Valley Isle. Wailuku and Kahului, close in size and geography but far apart philosophically, are natural rivals. Longtime residents are not timid about bragging up one of the towns and tearing down the other, depending on whose town is in question at the moment. But Kahului is not just ''business.'' Its shopping area is especially attractive and shows the results of planning a commercial area with people's esthetic pleasure in mind.

Wailuku's main street leads to a historically significant and especially beautiful valley about 3 miles to the west. Iao Valley is celebrated because it is here that in 1790 the all-conquering Kamehameha I established himself as the most powerful ruler in the Islands by defeating the forces of the king of Maui in a bloody battle. One of the more vivid tales about the carnage has it that so many Maui warriors fell that their bodies dammed up, and their blood reddened, Iao Stream which follows a rapid course through the valley. A well-known feature of green and quiet little Iao Valley is Iao Needle, a slender 2,250-foot point of volcanic rock carved by erosion and mantled in rich green, like the rest of this lush valley.

Lahaina, mentioned in the opening paragraphs of this section, is just 22 miles from Wailuku, on West Maui's coast. Though not a ''big city'' like the isthmian pair, Lahaina is far better known. It should be. Its history antedated the coming of the white man, whether he be whaler or missionary. Before Hawaii made its entry into western society, Kamehameha the Great made Lahaina his first capital after he had subdued Maui's chiefs. The mortal remains of some of the great names in early Hawaiian royalty lie in Lahaina's Wainee Cemetery, in a fragrant setting of multi-hued plumeria blooms. Lahaina has some of the oldest missionary-inspired buildings in the islands, including Lahainaluna High School, founded in 1831. The Old Baldwin House, built by missionaries in the early 1800s, and now a museum, is an instance of how those Boston worthies imported their own culture into the islands. It is a striking example of New England architecture.

Old Lahaina is giving a little ground to the new, in the form of the growing tourism that has reached this coast of Maui. But the town, in its picturesque setting between the sea and the mountains, is still an easy place to explore on foot. It's only about four blocks deep and stretches 2 miles along the waterfront (no beach). The growth of the Kaanapali-Napili resort areas just to the north have brought new shopping complexes to Lahaina, but the town's slow-moving, casual old-town air is not likely to change soon. It is consciously preserving its colorful past, and has been designated a National Historic Landmark.

The Kaanapali and Napili Bay coastal stretches just above Lahaina have become major tourist playgrounds. White sandy beaches and rocky coves such as those at the much-photographed Kapalua Bay mark this coast for even more extensive seaside development. Beyond Kapalua are more beaches, each with its own version of what a beach should offer, whether it be swimming, diving, surfing, or boating.

Past the beaches and around to the windward side of West Maui, the people and the roads thin out considerably. Civilization, western-style, has not made much of an impression on this part of Maui. Even the coast "highway" becomes a dirt track for 12 miles or so before reaching Waihee, four miles from Wailuku. Along the way is tiny Kahakuloa village, whose people live in much the same way they did in former times. Nowadays, however, the thatched roofs have been replaced by corrugated iron, and the simple lives of the villagers are rounded out by television-watching at night.

That large part of east Maui comprised of the slopes of Haleakala is called the Kula district. In this cool upland interior are cattle grazing lands and extensive fields of flowers and vegetables. This lovely and fertile area can be approached from either of the two towns on the isthmus, Kahului being the closer. "Friendly" and "restful" are descriptives often applied to this windward part of Maui where lush plant growth is the rule. Eucalyptus groves dot the green hillsides and perfume the soft air. Purple-blossomed jacaranda trees add spring-time color to the roadsides. Unmarked side roads offer opportunities for investigating in depth the charms of this gentle countryside.

The human contributions add an extra dimension to the uplands. House gardens display a dazzling variety of flowers, and the University of Hawaii maintains two agricultural experiment stations where new bedding plant varieties are a feast for the eye. One of these facilities is near the town of Makawao, itself a visual delight with its weathered wooden store fronts out of the "Old West." The Catholic Church of the Holy Ghost, a beautiful octagonal treasure build in 1897 mainly for Portuguese farm workers, sits aside the Kula Highway just under Haleakala's misty summit. Other churches add their graceful presence as well: St. John's Episcopal in Koekea, founded by a Chinese Lutheran minister; and the missionary-built Pookela Church of coral stone, near Olinda. Near the end of the Kula Highway (37) is a Hawaiian religious symbol, a sacred boulder. Legend says the lava rock was formerly a man who made the mistake of riling Pele, the volcano goddess. She did her thing, as usual.

The impulse toward tourism is accelerating the development of vacationers' pleasure-domes on Maui. Some are already established, as on West Maui's Kaanapali-Napili-Kapalua coastal strip. On others of Maui's sunny, silent beaches, the bulldozers are working or poised for the "go" signal to launch monster resort and residential communities. One of these, called Wailea Pua Kuleana, is already in the first stages of a proposed 20-year building program on a part of the coastal strip between Makena and Kihei. People are a natural part of the landscape, and accommodations have to be made for them. But too many people and too many accommodations could intrude upon the natural treasure that was the original reason for the development. We are slowly learning not to overwhelm the rest of nature with our admiration. Temperance in the rush for the tourist dollar will be essential to preserve the unique natural qualities of Maui for many future generations of man and his fellow creatures.

(Following Two Pages:) A Hawaiian sunset is like none other. This example is at Haena Pt., Kauai.

63

KAUAI

Kauai is the smallest of the four main islands. In area, it comes after Hawaii, Maui, and Oahu. If you count seven islands, including also Molokai, Lanai, and Niihau, then Kauai comes in the middle. Tiny Kahoolawe doesn't matter. It's barren, and uninhabited by human beings, and whatever other beings choose to live there have to duck the bombs and guns of the United States Navy, which uses it as a practice range.

Kauai's mere 553 square miles contain remarkably varied and beautiful terrain. Its nickname, ''Garden Island,'' is come by honestly. A combination of incredible torrents of rain and fertile soil have covered it with a green carpet of vegetation. Kauai's rich earth has had more time than that of the other islands to break down from its volcanic base. Waialeale, Kauai's volcanic creator and first mountain to emerge from the sea, was also the first Hawaiian furnace to shut down. As if to keep old Waialeale from starting up again, rains up to 600 inches a year pound it, more than enough to keep it quiet.

Little Kauai specializes in big contrasts. Its nearly circular coastline goes from very wet, cool, and green on the windward (north) coast to quite dry and warm on the lee side. Its topography ranges from the timbered slopes of rain-drenched Waialeale and its retinue of wooded valleys, to an extensive agricultural plain, to sunny beaches of crystalline white sand, to dramatic ridges of cliffs that stand in proud challenge to the ocean which created them. Battered by wind, rain, and the sea, Kauai's north coast seems an appropriate symbol of the self-reliant role Kauai has played in the Hawaiian segment of the islands' human history. In Kamahameha's forced unification of the islands, Kauai remained the only holdout, although its ruler, Kaumualii, later brought it into the Hawaiian kingdom.

Kauai's violent contrasts have fostered myths and legends that still have a strong hold on the imaginations of its people. One of these long-lived traditions concerns the *Menehune*, little, gnome-like people who, the legends say, were builders *extraordinaire*. Whenever something mysterious occurred in nature, like great rock movements, or earth slides that may have created dams, or even animal trails in the forest, the Menehune got the credit. The early Hawaiians were careful not to surprise the shy little wonder-workers at their tasks. They became violently unhappy if they caught someone watching.

Kauai is still sparsely inhabited, either permanently by residents or occasionally by jet-assisted tourists. A lot of the island is wild and rugged, not suitable for large numbers of humanity. Some of it, to be more accurate, is nearly unapproachable, still in its same wilderness state since before Kauai was discovered by Polynesians and, later, western explorers. The most formidable of these fastnesses is the Na Pali Coast to the northwest. No roads lead into or out of this line of cliffs, some of which tower 3,000 feet. Even a landing on the Na Pali beaches is a sometime thing. The sea swallows up the beach in winter and raging waves push in to the steep rock wall. In summer the elements are usually calmer, and swimming and fishing is possible. Only recently has man begun to penetrate this wild coast in appreciable numbers, and this has come about from the sky. Since the sixties, tourists and hunters have been dropped onto the Na Pali Coast from helicopters, more than 100,000 a year. One assumes they leave the same way.

An eleven-mile hiking and riding trail along this coast feeds into some of the few accessible valleys of the back country. The trail itself goes up and down like a roller coaster, but there are many rewards along its length. Starting from Haena at the end of the road on the north, there are caves to explore, long views of broad beaches, glimpses of the interior Na Pali country and its jungled valleys, and close encounters with pandanus and wild orchids. About halfway along the trail, at a spot where Hanakoa Stream cuts through, is a beautiful little pool with a waterfall. And toward the end of the trail is mile-long Kalalua Beach with both ''wet'' and dry caves. All of these coastal caves are said to be the work of the ubiquitous *Menehune*.

Famed Kalalua Valley is the culmination of the Na Pali Coast. It is completely enclosed in towering cliffs and contains the ruins of ancient Hawaiian villages. The area is remembered in legend as the hideout of Koolau the leper, who eluded (and shot) pursuers intent on sending him to the leper colony on Molokai. South of Kalalua is the Kokee Plateau, much of it now a state park. Until quite recently these highlands were shielded from civilization by an almost impenetrable tropical rain forest. Now several roads wander through it, although only one, route 55, is paved. Route 55 enters Kokee from Waimea Canyon State Park to the south and continues on to the plateau's northeastern extremity at Kalalau Lookout, a lofty vantage point where the overpowering splendor of the Na Pali Coast is within eye's reach.

The Alakai Swamp is part of the Kokee region. Alakai is not a swamp at all in the usual sense. The swampy designation refers to Alakai's heavy rainfall rather than to a drainage problem. About the only pathway to Alakai is a trail from Waimea State Park. Alakai's unique character is now generally recognized. It's a 20-square-mile wilderness bog in a forest preserve and supports species of bird and plant life found nowhere else in the world. National Parks Magazine (March 1967) says it is ''rich in species of sedges, flowers, and many lobelias . . Three species of birds, the Kauai creeper, akialoa, and nukupuu . . . ''

Another Kauai ''spectacular'' cuts into the Kokee plateau on the south. Waimea Canyon lures thousands of visitors to Kauai on its own merits. Waimea is an almost 3,000-foot-deep chasm that cuts into Kokee Plateau, and its formations remind one of the Grand Canyon, although all of Waimea could fit into a very small fraction of the mainland canyon. Compact as it is, it stands front and center before the eye in all its glory. What makes Waimea especially memorable is its range of colors, caused by the presence of extensive vegetation in addition to the volcanic rock monoliths and canyon walls. Clouds hanging around the canyon's rim keep changing the values of the blues, greens, reds, and browns, and their moving shadows on the canyon structures add to the rich kaleidoscope of Waimea.

Barking Sands is a noisy curiosity at Mana on the west coast. The white coral sand is piled up in dunes, some 60 feet high. When the wind blows, on dry days, the moving sand produces a sound which sounds something like a far-off bark. One can stir up a big racket by sliding down one of the dunes. And rubbing the stuff between the palms, or simply walking on it, will produce the sounds. According to a Hawaiian legend concerning this phenomenon, a popular chieftain was slain in a great battle on this spot, and ever since, the sands have groaned.

By following the coastline, the further discovery of Kauai's variety becomes routine. The south shore, from Koloa to Polihale, is much drier than the windward side, and is also warmer and less green. There are some good swimming and surfing beaches near Koloa, including the tourist hotels that spring up where sand and sun are mixed in the desired

(Left Page Above:) Lehua in flower on pahoehoe lava; right, plumeria blooms. Below, an Oriental garden in Maui's Iao Valley.

(Reading clockwise, from top left:) Torch ginger, orchid, hanging heliconia, wild Madagascar periwinkle.

proportion. Poipu Beach is one such place. More important from a cultural standpoint are the colorful old west buildings of the towns like Koloa and Hanapepe, the Japanese and Hawaiian religious shrines and artifacts, remains of a Russian fort at Waimea, and Kauai's oldest mission (1820), also at Waimea. For pure appreciation there are the botanical gardens of Kauai, the finest in all the islands. The gardens, such as Plantation Gardens at Poipu Beach and Menehune Garden at Nawiliwili (to the east), are nearly all open to visitors. Countless varieties of tropical species are grown under controlled conditions and include food and medicinal plants and sumptuous orchid and hibiscus displays such as those at Olu Pua Gardens on the heights at Kalaheo.

The small town of Lihue is Kauai's principal ''city.'' It still has an old-town appearance, but a new look is emerging. Many new residences and public buildings have been completed in recent years, including a good museum where Kauai's history is covered by extensive displays.

Kauai's windward coast, from Haena on the north to Lihue, has an abundance of natural charm, relics of former settlements, and few people. The north coast is populated mostly by legends and those mythical *Menehune*; it is rich in caves, coves, bays, and cliffs; where the road ends just west of Haena, there's a lovely merger of sea and sand called Ke'e Beach. On Haena's other side are the eminently photogenic Lumahai and Hanalei bays. Lumahai's beach, a soft crescent of white sand fringed by pandanus, gets its picture taken more than almost any other Hawaiian beach. Hanalei is beloved by filmmakers for its photogenic qualities; *South Pacific* was filmed here, as were other south seas epics. One of the film companies' legacies is Hanalei Plantation, a hotel that hangs on the heights above the bay, and where a room with a view is not hard to find.

Taro fields and truck farms are much in evidence along this part of the coast between Hanalei and Kilauea. Kalihiwai Bay, near Kilauea, is notorious for having been visited by a killer tidal wave in 1946. A small village on its shore is testimony to the natives' confidence in an early warning system that now watches the oceans for such seismic disturbances. Further east, around the bend of the coast, is Anahola, a little ''country'' place in the traditional sleepy mold. Near Anahola on the seaward side is Anahola Bay, with its ''hole-in-the-mountain'' cliff. A legend explains the situation: a spear was thrown with such force that a hole was blasted in the rock wall. There's some disagreement as to the thrower — one story gives credit to a giant; another implicates Kamehameha I himself, who missed when he aimed the spear at an enemy.

The coastal strip from Anahola to Kapaa is especially scenic, with lush coastal valleys cutting into the mountain ridges. This area, notably Kapaa, has some beautiful and interesting churches, including Episcopal, Mormon, Catholic, Adventist, and Buddhist. It also has, below Kapaa and near Wailua Beach, a large tourist complex called Coco Palms, a veteran among Kauai resorts. Inland of the highway, between Kapaa and Wailua, is a mountain profile that is a tour guide's favorite. Called the Sleeping Giant, it appears to have shaped itself into a sleeping figure.

Just a few miles north of Lihue is the Wailua·River area, now Wailua River State Park, where recreation and history are closely blended. Some of the history is symbolized by the ruins of a temple of refuge, where in former times, fugitives were safe from capture. Some of the recreation is available in a short boat trip up the Wailua River to the famed Fern Grotto, rich in scenic and folkloric qualities. The river banks on the way are thickly covered with pandanus, *hau*, and *pili* grass. The Grotto itself is a fern-hung cave at the end of a short jungle trail. An amphitheater, it is used as a sounding board by some Hawaiian singers whenever a boatload of tourists visits the place. It's unclear why people, even in Hawaii, would stand around in a cool, dark, damp cave just for the opportunity to bring music to visitors. They may really be grown-up Menehune, the little people who used to turn mere mortals to stone just for looking at them . . . perhaps belatedly trying to live down their reputation for unsocial behavior.

Anything can happen on the very magical island of Kauai.

PHOTO CREDITS

Ray Atkeson: *page 13, top; page 16-17; page 26, bottom; page 29, top; page 31; page 34, top; page 38, top; page 40, top; page 44, top; page 44, bottom; page 46, top; page 50, bottom; page 52; page 53, bottom; page 60, bottom; page 68, bottom; page 69, top left.*

David Muench: *page 9; page 12; page 13, bottom; page 20-21; page 24, top; page 24, bottom; page 25; page 27; page 28; page 29, bottom; page 30; page 32-32; page 34, bottom; page 35; page 36-37; page 38, bottom; page 39; page 40, bottom; page 41; page 42; page 43, top; page 43, bottom; page 45; page 46, bottom; page 47; page 48-49; page 50, top; page 51; page 53, top; page 54, top; page 54, bottom; page 55; page 56; page 57, top; page 57, bottom; page 60, top; page 61; page 64-65; page 68, top left; page 68, top right; page 69, top right; page 69, bottom left; page 69, bottom right; page 72.*

(Following Page:)
Akaka Falls, near Hilo, has its own state park, a tropical forest setting where a variety of vegetation flourishes. Surrounding the heliconia bloom here are tree fern, taro, and ti plants.